THE
Thing
that
Mattered
MOST

THE
Thing
that
Mattered
MOST

Scottish poems for children

Preface by Michael Morpurgo

Edited by Julie Johnstone

Illustrated by Iain McIntosh

Scottish Poetry Library · Black & White Publishing

First published in 2006 by

SCOTTISH POETRY LIBRARY
5 Crichton's Close, Edinburgh EH8 8DT
www.spl.org.uk

and

BLACK & WHITE PUBLISHING
99 Giles Street, Edinburgh EH6 6BZ
www.blackandwhitepublishing.com

ISBN 13   978 1 84502 095 8
ISBN 10   1 84502 095 2

SCOTTISH EXECUTIVE

Supported by
The National Lottery®
through the Scottish Arts Council

Scottish
Arts Council

Designed by Iain McIntosh

Printed and bound in Poland www.polskabook.pl

Mixed Sources
Product group from well-managed
forests and other controlled sources
www.fsc.org Cert no. SGS–COC–2086
© 1996 Forest Stewardship Council

This book is printed on Arctic the Volume 115 g/m².
Arctic Paper is a holder of FSC traceability certificate.

Dedicated to a poet
who matters enormously,
EDWIN MORGAN
first Scots Makar

c o n t

e n t s

in my family

in my head

afterword

preface

THIS IS ALL VERY STRANGE. Here I am, not a poet, not a Scot, yet I've been invited to write an introduction to a book of poems by Scottish poets. I want to tell you why I was so happy to be asked, so happy to do it.

Although I'm English, I've always been very connected to Scotland, to Scottish poetry and Scottish children. Scottish history has always fascinated me too – from Robert the Bruce to the Clearances. And I've written stories about Scotland. I've done extensive reading tours all over, from the Western Isles to St Andrews, in towns and cities, in island schools, in village halls. I love Scotland, mostly, I think, because of two men, two of my literary heroes, both Scots unlike me, both poets, unlike me. One I 'met' as a child and grew up with. He was, and still is, the writer I most want to be. Here was a man who in his short life wrote poetry and travel books, marvellous adventure stories and great novels. The other was a man I knew well, a dear friend, who lived until his death in a cottage just down the lane from me in Devon.

Robert Louis Stevenson is the writer I have always most wanted to be. Here's a man who can compose and paint, only he uses words. Like no other writer I've known, he makes words sing. I first came across him as a seven-year-old when I was given *Treasure Island* to read. I wasn't a great reader at the time, and I think I only began to read it because I liked the bloodthirsty pirate illustrations. But once I began to read it was no longer the pictures that interested me. Stevenson played his tune and like the Pied Piper led me into his story. I was entranced at once, all disbelief instantly suspended. Why? Because he could draw characters as surely as landscape, because through the power of his storytelling, he could make me feel I was right there inside the story. I was Jim Hawkins hiding inside that barrel of apples on the ship, the *Hispaniola*. Trembling I heard every word the despicable, dastardly Long John Silver spoke. I was the hidden witness to his dreadful conspiracy. Get caught and I'd have my throat cut.

Later *Kidnapped* introduced me to Scottish

Farewell to the Farm

The coach is at the door at last;
The eager children, mounting fast
And kissing hands, in chorus sing:
Good-bye, good-bye, to everything!

To house and garden, field and lawn,
The meadow-gates we swang upon,
To pump and stable, tree and swing,
Good-bye, good-bye, to everything!

And fare you well for evermore,
O ladder at the hayloft door,
O hayloft where the cobwebs cling,
Good-bye, good-bye, to everything!

Crack goes the whip, and off we go;
The trees and houses smaller grow;
Last, round the woody turn we swing:
Good-bye, good-bye, to everything!

history, and *Travels with a Donkey*, to France, and to donkeys. And my mother used to read me his poetry. Great poetry touches your heart, opens your eyes, explores fear and doubt, joy and love.

On my farm in Devon, over the last thirty years, we have had thousands of city children to stay for a while, a class at a time with their teachers. When they leave after maybe the happiest week of their young lives, they are sad. Watching the coach go off down the lane, I often think of Stevenson's wonderful poem, 'Farewell to the Farm'.

Seán Rafferty, my second Scottish poet hero, although brought up in the Borders and in Edinburgh, lived most of his life in Devon. I never knew a man more connected to the people and the countryside around him. Like Stevenson, he too wrote song poems. He had a great ear for the music of words, for rhythm and rhyme, and he too could paint pictures with his pen. 'From Hereabout Hill' is a picture, a picture poem, a song poem, he made about the valley where I live.

And here is a whole book of Scottish poems. They come from the world of Robert Louis Stevenson and Seán Rafferty and Rabbie Burns, and George Mackay Brown and Sorley MacLean, and because they're great poems they are universal poems, for me, for you, for everyone.

From Hereabout Hill

From Hereabout Hill
the sun early rising
looks over his fields
where a river runs by;
at the green of the wheat
and the green of the barley
and Candlelight Meadow
the pride of his eye.

The clock on the wall
strikes eight in the kitchen
the clock in the parlour
says twenty to nine;
the thrush has a song
and the blackbird another
the weather reporter
says cloudless and fine.

It's green by the hedge
and white by the peartree
in Hereabout village
the date is today;
it's seven by the sun
and the time is the springtime
the first of the month and
the month must be May.

I'VE LOVED READING EVERY ONE of them. But please, do one thing for me: read them out loud. Children, they used to say, should be seen but not heard. Well, poetry I reckon needs to be heard, not just seen. Speak it out and you can feel the music of it. Above all poetry should be felt.

MICHAEL MORPURGO

Kiss

For want of a mountain a primrose was lost,

For want of a primrose a love song was lost,

For want of a love song a sly kiss was lost,

And that was the thing that mattered most,

Yes, that was the thing that mattered most.

Robert Crawford

Robert Crawford I was born in Lanarkshire in 1959 and now live in St Andrews where I am Professor of Modern Scottish Literature in the School of English at the university. One of the things I love most about poetry is the way it can pattern sounds and rhythms to make music in spoken language; my poem in this anthology tries to do that.

THE THING THAT MATTERED MOST...

in the water...

Flip flotsam

This is the beach
where the flip flops come
at the end of their
flip flop trip.

And where does a
flip flop trip begin?

> the floor of a flip flop factory;
> on the shelf of a flip flop shop;
> or the foot of a flip flop fan?

And what snaps the strap
of each flip flop
that finds its flip flop fate?

> a flip too far;
> a flop too fast;
> or a slip that
> flapped it back?

And what does the sea say
when she sees another flip flop fall?

'Oh, flip flop and flotsam
fair and foul,
I'll freely float you all!'?

Or, do the waters, wavy and wide,
curse each clutch of clutter
that comes on each tide
and storms up the sand
with curses that worsen
at each
beach-tripping
     strap-snapping
         flip-flopping person?

Elspeth Murray

Elspeth Murray I was brought up in Blairgowrie and now live in Edinburgh with my husband Richard Medrington who is a poet and a puppeteer. Together we have published *The Eel's Eyebrows*, a collection of nonsense poetry by children. I wrote 'Flip Flotsam' on a beach in Kenya in 1997. It inspired a film of the same name that describes the lifecycle of flip-flops and shows an amazing recycling project where flip-flops are turned into jewellery and toys – crazy but true!

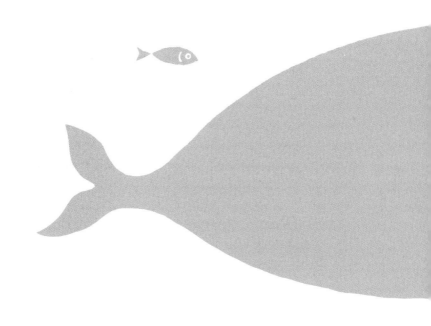

it was *this* big!
the child tells her mother,
on the phone

Alan Spence

Alan Spence I was born in Glasgow, live in Edinburgh and teach at the University of Aberdeen. I write novels and plays as well as wee poems like this one – just catching a moment that made me smile and will maybe make the reader smile too.

Five fish

1 THIS ONE SEEMED TO BE HAPPY ON GRAVEL.
Sipping flies down to
her very own stones.

One day she fell with the current
all the way to the wide sea.

And then she's hunting shrimps and prawns,
all that pink going deep inside.
The muscle tight but slim as a rocket,
the shine broken with beads of black.

Till she and her mates have turned around
thirsty for remembered water
that's just around the
next narrowing

so she swims until
she bruises her belly.

2 THIS ONE PLAYS THE WATER LIKE WINE.
The high fin is long and a sail
so it swims in a spiral.
As a cork is unturned
from the cloudy neck
of a thick bottle.

The silver of salt
in fresh water.

The one that livens up when
the slowing chill is on the river.

3 THIS DART IS CERTAIN AND SHARP
but has fifteen spines
on its back.

You can see through shape
to see the hairy bones
bristle inside.

4 THIS ONE HOVERS
striped by reeds
– a shark in a lake.

He's made of marble
and gorgonzola.
Heavy as butter.

Pivots like a stuntbike
and rhymes with one too.

5 THIS BACK CAN SHOW A KITE
filling, pulling
round quiet water.

A tiger in olive and green
accelerating to
a flash of lipstick red.

Ian Stephen

Ian Stephen I was born on the Isle of Lewis, outer Hebrides, and still live there. I've written poems about my own childhood, close to the harbour in Stornoway, and about visits to my father's hometown of Fraserburgh. Fish and fishing have always been part of my life. This poem was written for a friend, David Graham, who set it to music. It was performed by a Russian children's choir in Bonn in 2005.

1. SALMON   2. GRAYLING   3. 15-SPINED STICKLEBACK   4. PIKE   5. PERCH

coire fhionn lochan

lapping of the little waves
breaking of the little waves
spreading of the little waves
idling of the little waves

rippling of the little waves
settling of the little waves
meeting of the little waves
swelling of the little waves

trembling of the little waves
dancing of the little waves
pausing of the little waves
slanting of the little waves

tossing of the little waves
scribbling of the little waves
lilting of the little waves
sparkling of the little waves

leaping of the little waves
drifting of the little waves
running of the little waves
splashing of the little waves

Thomas A. Clark

Thomas A. Clark I was born in Greenock and now live on the east coast in the fishing village of Pittenweem. My poems are often written on walks in the highlands and islands. They may be about spending time quietly in a wood or, like the poem above, watching the movement of the waves on a little loch on the island of Arran. Like the waves on a loch, each line of the poem is only slightly different from all the others.

just another pebble

don't get me wrong
        i have nothing
against roundness
        as a concept;

it's just
        that
i should like to have
some interesting angles.

the others,
        those look-alikes?
they're all washed up!

see
i have this streak
        in me.

i could show you
        some interesting
facets
        if i wanted to.

sometimes

        i feel
i could just break out
        in rhomboidal
planes & polyhedra

if i weren't
        rubbing shoulders

    with this lot.

Eunice M. Buchanan

Eunice M. Buchanan I was born and brought up in Arbroath on the east coast of Scotland. Just north of Arbroath, there is a wonderful pebble beach where many of the pebbles are very similar — smooth and rounded — because they have been rubbing up against one another in the swirling tides. I like writing poetry because sometimes a poem will try to tell me something that I didn't know I was thinking about.

How many sailors to sail a ship?

One with a broken heart
to weep sad buckets.

Two with four blue eyes
to mirror the sea.

One with a salty tongue
to swear at a pirate.

Two with four green eyes
to mirror the sea.

One with a wooden leg
to dance on a gangplank.

Two with four grey eyes
to mirror the sea.

Luff! Leech! Clew! Tack!
Off to sea! Won't be back!

One with an arrowed heart

tattooed on a bicep.

Two with four blue eyes
to mirror the sky.

One with a baby's caul
to keep from a-drowning.

Two with four grey eyes
to mirror the sky.

One with a flask of rum
to gargle at midnight.

Two with four black eyes
to mirror the sky.

Luff! Clew! Tack! Leech!
Off to sea! No more beach!

One with an albatross
to put in a poem.

Two with four blue eyes
to mirror the sea.

One with a secret map
to stitch in a lining.

Two with four grey eyes
to mirror the sea.

One with a violin
to scrape at a dolphin.

Two with four green eyes
to mirror the sea.

Luff! Leech! Tack! Clew!
Off to sea! Yo ho! Adieu!

One with a telescope
to clock the horizon.

Two with four blue eyes
to mirror the sky.

One with a yard of rope
to lasso a tempest.

Two with four grey eyes
to mirror the sky.

One with a heavy heart
to sink for an anchor.

Two with four black eyes
to mirror the sky.

Leech! Clew! Tack! Luff!
Off to sea! We've had enough!

Carol Ann Duffy

Carol Ann Duffy I was born in Glasgow and my books include *Meeting Midnight*, *The Oldest Girl in the World* and *The Good Child's Guide to Rock 'n' Roll*. I was on holiday in Aberdovey with my ten-year-old daughter, Ella. We were sitting on a roof bar overlooking the sea and she asked me, 'How many sailors does it take to sail a ship?' So I wrote this poem.

In the SKY

Scottish rain

Gets in yer neb, lugs,
unner thi oxters tae.
Oan yer heid, in yer een
til ye're drookit, ken?

An it's aye cauld
an gaes sidie-ways.
Whit, warm rain?
Nae here (mebbe in Spain).

Woke up this mornin,
crawled oot o bed,
keeked oot thi windae pane
Aw naw! Rainin again!

Tom Bryan

Tom Bryan I was born in Canada but now live in Kelso in the Scottish Borders. I wrote the poem this way because I like the way Scottish words best describe Scottish things, like rain! I often write with paper and pencil, sitting in front of a window, looking outside at whatever the weather is doing. I became a poet because I like to make sense of what I see, think or hear and that's what poetry tries to do.

Murder of crows

We're the best dressed here.
Forget the scruffy starlings
dishevelled thrushes
the gaudy tits and finches –
they're all a waste of space.

We're the real class act:
never a feather out of place
our blacks perfectly matched.
Like gangsters, ministers,
we demand respect.

Our quills drink in the light
like ink.

Dilys Rose

Dilys Rose I grew up in Glasgow, have lived in Edinburgh for many years and like to travel when I can. I have written one book of poems for young children, *When I Wear My Leopard Hat*. I wrote this poem as part of a sequence based on collective nouns, that is names for groups of animals or people. Some of these names are very old and many seem strange today, e.g. Skulk of Foxes, Lamentation of Swans, Neverthriving of Jugglers, Blessing of Unicorns (all of which I've written about). I wanted to use the strangeness of the names as a starting point for the poems.

Wren

A tidy wren, tiny apron on,

spot-checks the garden.

Not a speck –

she's gone.

Richard Price

Richard Price I grew up in Renfrewshire, just southwest of Glasgow. That was in those days pretty much the countryside but I didn't see a wren all the time I was there. Then, a couple of years ago, one flew into the garden of the city flat where I now live. Before I could think, 'This is one of the tiniest, most beautiful birds I have ever seen', it had gone.

Pass the word

I'm a protectit bird.

They're settin girns for vermin

Like stoats and their kin;

The fox is huntit and shot doon

And aw to keep me safe and soon.

Pass the word

I'm a protectit bird.

You micht say august

And that is surely just.

Aw is for my health

And a pairty on the twelfth!

Duncan Glen

Duncan Glen I was born in Cambuslang, Lanarkshire, and now live in Kirkcaldy in Fife. As a boy, I lived near coal mines and steelworks but these were in pleasant green fields and near the River Clyde, so I knew the farmlands and woods well and my poems on birds are based on memories of my boyhood. They were written for my children.

Captain Puggle

Captain Puggle flees his plane
Frae Tumshie Airport tae Bahrain
Gets the Smiths and their wee wean
Brings them aw back hame again.

Captain Puggle flees tae Barra
Skites aff like a shootin arra
But he'll soon be back the morra
Pechin like a puggled sparra.

Captain Puggle's oot o ile
Efter ainly twinty mile
Sae he has tae bide a while
In a field ootside Carlisle.

Captain Puggle jets tae Crete
Wi his neebor, Bowfer Pete
In the cockpit, Bowfer's feet
Aye mak Captain Puggle greet.

Captain Puggle's sellt his plane
Says he'll never flee again
But next week he's aff tae Spain
In his brand-new Buhlitt Train.

Matthew Fitt

Matthew Fitt I am a Dundonian. I have poems in *King o the Midden* and *Blethertoun Braes*. I wrote 'Captain Puggle' in honour of a man called Mirek who has a plane and likes to fly it upside down and in bad weather just to scare everyone. I could have called the poem 'Captain Mirek' but Puggle is a much better name for a mad pilot.

So, what if everybody's feet left from a plan

lumino

then, THEN, look down from

lines of light that wander about an

and criss

and cross

and THEN you'd kno

Journeys

ght, at night and you'd see these

acks like, you know, snails do,

and stock still

and start up and turn around again

lot about journeys?

Maybe not. But wouldn't it look WICKED!

Joan Lennon

Joan Lennon I was born in Canada but I've spent the best half of my life living in Fife. My books include *Questors* and *The Ely Plot* (the first book of *The Wickit Chronicles*). I like poems with strange shapes, where the words go sideways and upside down or maybe even cross in the middle!

Little star

Little star, so far, so near,
I see your eye's one shining tear.

Little star, so wild, so tame,
I waved my hand. You never came.

Little star, so quick, so slow,
you whisper like the drifting snow.

Little star, so dark, so deep
the sea you swim in as I sleep.

When morning comes in like the tide
you will have reached the other side.

Swim, star, swim, through the midnight sea
(when your hair is dry, come back to me!)

Little star, so near, so far,
shine on Wick and Zanzibar

on Dundee, Belfast and Aragh,
and shine on my bike's bent handlebar

shine like its silver bell
                    dring dring
        shine like its silver bell
                    and sing
            sharp as a silver bell.

James McGonigal

James McGonigal I was born and grew up in Dumfries in the southwest of Scotland but now live in Glasgow. When my four children were small, I used to make up stories and rhymes for them and I have published poems in Scots for children in the Itchy Coo series. This particular poem was written when I was working with some primary teachers on the classroom topic of 'The Moon and the Stars'.

in the country...

The twa cuddies

As I cam roon by Tinto's back,
I heard twa cuddies haein a crack.
I heard yin tae the tither say,
'Wha will ye tak tae ride the-day?'

'I'll tak nae laird wi whip and spurs,
I'll tak nae leddy clad in furs.
But I'll awa tae Glesca fair
Tae fetch a lass that I ken there.

'And nane will hear me at the gate,
And nane will see me as I wait
But her alane, and she'll come doun,
And we'll gang through the sleepin toun.

'We'll ride the bents, we'll ride the braes,
We'll ride for nichts, we'll ride for days.
We'll ride the shore, we'll ride the sea,
We'll ride the sky, that lass and me.'

As I wis sittin late at nicht
Abune the trees I saw a sicht:
Across the mune I saw them pass,
A fleein cuddy and a lass.

James Robertson

James Robertson I stay in Angus, about ten miles north of Dundee. Along with Matthew Fitt, I have written or edited several books in Scots, all published by Itchy Coo. These include *A Moose in the Hoose*, *A Wee Book o Fairy Tales*, *Blethertoun Braes*, *King o the Midden* and *The Smoky Smirr o Rain*. 'The twa cuddies' is a kind of dream poem, written for a physically disabled friend who loved horses but was never able to ride one. It's based on an old ballad called 'The Twa Corbies'.

March weather

Wind in pines
wind on water
wind in rushes
wind on feather

Sun in leaves
sun on loch
sun in reeds
sun on duck

Rain in trees
rain on river
rain in moss
rain on eider

All one morning
all together
in an hour
March weather

Tessa Ransford

Tessa Ransford I was born in India, returning with my family at the age of ten to Scotland where I have lived most of my life since. Although I love poetry and children and have eight grandchildren, I don't often make a poem specifically for children but certainly hope they will enjoy many of my poems. I often walk in the Scottish countryside and this poem was written after a windy, sunny, rainy walk in the Rothiemurchus forest one March day.

Listening to the trees

And the birch says
            it's about dancing and colour
and the rowan says
            it's about berries and birds
and the willow says
            it's about shape and shelter
and the hazel says
            it's about love and lichen
and the aspen says
            it's about growth and the wind
but I say it's about
            listening to the trees

Mandy Haggith

Mandy Haggith I live on a coastal woodland croft in Assynt in the far northwest corner of Scotland. A wee collection of my nature poems, called *letting light in*, was published in 2005. I love trees, get inspiration from their different characters and moods, and I often find that sitting under a tree is the best place to write a poem.

The pluffman

'What is a pluffman?' – question by a French woman.

A pluffman is a man whose pluff
Is not quite sharp enough
To slice the soil like the shining blade
Of the genuine plough, on the winter days.

A pluffman's not a rough man
And certainly not a tough man
Nor (usually) a gruff man.
He fears he may be a duff man,
Poor pluffman,
One of a kind.

While on each field bright tractors go
The pluffman just looks down at his pluff
And shakes his head. He can huff and puff,
It'll make no difference. Who made this pluff,
He asks himself, out of such useless stuff?
He can't get started, even. The hopeless pluff
Sits and gazes at him with one bright eye,
Incurious creature with a thick buff ruff
Made out of fluff, and its only sound is – wuff.
And that is why
I made the poor pluffman this poem to live in –
He'd not get far in the actual world.
The pluffman's pluff is not plough enough.

Gerry Cambridge

Gerry Cambridge Until I was thirty-seven, I had never lived in a house. I had only ever lived in a caravan.
Now I live in a house not far outside Glasgow. I wrote 'The pluffman' after an ex-girlfriend, who was French,
looked up from a book she was reading and said, 'What is a pluffman?' (You must imagine her beautiful
accent.) 'Here, let me see,' I said. The word in the book was 'ploughman'. But having been introduced to the
pluffman, I decided I'd better find out about him.

From a landscape in April

Snowflake grinds against snowflake.
Grass creaks like old furniture.

I spread silence on the fields.

I bring home thick squares of it
to hang on my noisy walls.

Robin Fulton

Robin Fulton The first half of my life so far has been spent in Scotland and the second half in Norway, with frequent crossings of the North Sea. 'Why do you write poems?' is a question I can't really answer but I do know that many poems start as a kind of doodling, with words and with ideas, and then perhaps something falls into place. The poems I like best are like the people I like best – they are able to be a bit playful and a bit serious at the same time.

What the horses see at night

When the day-birds have settled
in their creaking trees,
the doors of the forest open
for the flitting
drift of deer
among the bright croziers
of new ferns
and the legible stars;
foxes stream from the earth;
a tawny owl
sweeps the long meadow.
In a slink of river-light,
the mink's face
is already slippery with yolk,
and the bay's
tiny islands are drops
of solder
under a drogue moon.
The sea's a heavy sleeper,
dreaming in and out with a catch

in each breath, and is not disturbed
by that *plowt* – the first
in a play of herring, a shoal
silvering open
the sheeted black skin of the sea.
Through the starting rain, the moon
skirrs across the sky dragging
torn shreds of cloud behind.
The fox's call is red
and ribboned
in the snow's white shadow.
The horses watch the sea climb
and climb and walk
towards them on the hill,
hear the vole
crying under the alder,
our children
breathing slowly in their beds.

Robin Robertson

Robin Robertson I was born in Scone, Perthshire, and brought up in Aberdeen. I have published three
collections of poetry. I live in London now but can't write there so I go on retreat to the country – ideally by
the sea – and spend my time walking and watching. This poem appeared after a long walk I took from dusk
to dawn, seeing the natural world come alive as the human world slept.

53

Poem

Rags frae the moon and tatters o sun,

We'll fly awa when time is done.

Wind for a sark; the sweet yird for shoon.

Rags frae the sun; tatters o moon.

John Glenday

John Glenday I live in an old cottage in the shadow of Cawdor Castle, near Inverness. I have been writing for longer than I can remember. Strangely enough, I tend to be happiest writing poems about the things that are so beautiful they make me sad. I wrote this poem for my small son, Matthias, after we had watched a full moon sail high over the woods one windy night in the late autumn.

in the wild...

A wolf in the park

Is there a wolf,
A wolf in the park,
A wolf who wakes when the night gets dark?
Is there a wolf in the park?

Is there a wolf,
A wolf who creeps
From his hidden den while the city sleeps?
Is there a wolf in the park?

Is there a wolf,
Whose nightly track
Circles the park fence, zigzags back?
Is there a wolf in the park?

Is there a wolf,
Who pads his way
Between the tables of the closed café,
Is there a wolf in the park?

Is there a wolf,
A wolf whose bite
Left those feathers by the pond last night,
Is there a wolf in the park?

Is there a wolf?
No one knows,
But I've heard a howl when the full moon glows . . .
Is there a wolf in the park?

Richard Edwards

Richard Edwards I was born in Kent and have lived in Edinburgh for the last fifteen years. I have written over thirty books for children, mostly collections of poetry and picture books, including *Teaching the Parrot* and *The Very Best of Richard Edwards*. I like poems about wild animals and this one came from thinking about what might be out there in the dark while the city dreams. In my imagination, the wolf in this poem might (or might not) be prowling around Inverleith Park or the Edinburgh Botanics at night – or in any other park near you. That's the good thing about poems – anything can happen in them . . .

Owl

Still hanging around, old boot face?
Old tin-can body with feathers.
Two decorative googly specs.
Two stumpy legs, all claw.

Right.

You're just the sort:
long on silence, short on talk.

(the woods at night seen sideways
the breeze in surreptitious feathers
the swoop and grab
the devouring)

We all know what you do with a detail.
You swallow it whole.
Days later we find it, cranked out:
a pair of sad little feet and some fur.

Not for you,
the easeful slide into verse.
Not for you.

A bird of *another* feather
altogether.

Ca canny. Ca canny. Ca canny.

Fiona Wilson

Fiona Wilson I grew up near Aberdeen and now live in New York City. I started writing poetry as a child and just never stopped. This poem began with an etching, by the artist John Bellamy, of a very fierce and sneaky-looking owl but it soon turned into a poem about the fierce and sneaky act of writing itself.

Deer

as crows fly
in the dawn light
on the cold hill
the deer are running

the thud of their hooves
on the bed of the stream
is the drum that rocks
the roots of the birch
and the wind that shakes
the birch tree's leaves

rain is their tribe song
rain is their robe

snow is the dust
of the bones of deer
falling to earth

and earth is the dark
deep silence of things
where you dream yourself
human, alive
watching the red deer running
on the wall of a cave

Chris Powici

Chris Powici I live in Dunblane. Animals of all kinds, from blue tits to grey seals, are a big part of my writing. I wrote 'Deer' after seeing a herd of deer on a mountainside in the Highlands. The sight of these stunning creatures made me think about how they have featured in all kinds of stories and poems down the years. In the end, I was left with the image of cave paintings of deer and I knew that these 'ancient' deer had to go in my poem along with the ones I had seen roaming among the grass and heather.

Wild

Today,
on our journey home,
we saw

a buzzard
making a kill
on the roadside verge.

It glided across
our windscreen
and hunkered down

on something –
we couldn't see
what it was – as the wings

folded around
what Lucas called
'the prey'.

He wanted to know
if buzzards took children,
or cats;

then,
as we slowed to look,
he chose to admire

the plumage
and the fierce light
of its eye.

John Burnside

John Burnside I live in East Fife, outside Arncroach, in buzzard country. I was born in West Fife, in the coal mining town of Cowdenbeath. I've always been interested in birds and like to spend time these days watching the buzzards with my son, who is five. We saw this buzzard swoop down on to the verge when we were driving home one day and we stopped to watch it feed – the car was right next to where it was but it didn't care. That's one good thing about cars, I suppose – they are like mobile hides so you can see things from a car sometimes that you might not have seen otherwise. I once saw an Arctic fox up close, when I stopped my car and got out to stretch my legs, in northern Norway. They're quite shy and it's hard to get close to them but I was lucky enough to see it very close up – a beautiful moment.

Woolly bear

Woolly, woolly bear
Who feeds on the weeds,
Hurry furry chestnut,
Move at speed.

Wee hairy wobat
Warming in the sun,
On curlywurly loops
Many feet run.

By dandelion and nettle
Wriggly-squiggly crawl,
When you are touched,
Curl up in a ball.

Woolly, woolly bear,
Ginger-beer froth,
Vanish and change
Into a tiger moth.

Valerie Gillies

Valerie Gillies Sometimes I write in my hut in an Edinburgh garden but this poem began halfway up a hill after a steep climb. The woolly bear caterpillar I saw among long green grasses near a spring of clear water. Nearly all my poems begin with something I see outdoors on a walk and think, 'That's it!'

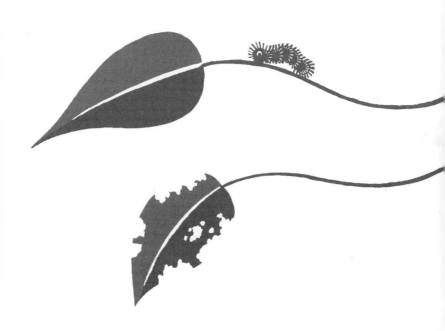

Bully Cat

Bully Cat
is very fat
and smelly

his body
is mostly
his belly

Bully Cat
is lazy
and nasty

lying down
he's like a crazy
Cornish pasty

Bully Cat
despises
his owner

he eats her food
but deep down
he's a loner

Bully Cat
is very far
from housetrained

and further still
from bird-trained
or mouse-trained

for Bully Cat
will go where
he pleases

and every time
he kills something
he teases!

Bully Cat
is merciless
to other cats

to smaller cats
and kitten cats
and mother cats

and as for dogs,
well, Bully Cat
dismisses them!

he spits them
he claws them
he hisses them!

Bully Cat
tattoos those
who mess with him

so children tend
to play less
and less with him

Bully Cat
bit a girl
who kissed him

he died last week
and no one
missed him

Richard Medrington

Richard Medrington I was born near Liverpool and live in Edinburgh with my wife Elspeth Murray and our fat but gentle cat Tibor. As well as writing and performing poems, I work as a puppeteer in schools and theatres. 'Bully Cat' was inspired by an unusually fierce tabby I once knew. Writing this poem has helped me get over the experience but Tibor is still having counselling.

The chaffinch map of Scotland

chaffinch
chaffinchaffinch
chaffinchaffinchaffinch
chaffinchaffinchaffinch
chaffinchaffinch
chaffinch
chaffie   chye   chaffiechaffie
chaffie   chye   chaffiechaffie
chye chaffie
chaffiechaffiechaffie
chaffiechaffiechaffie
chaffiechaffie
chaffiechaffie
chaffiechaffie
chaffiechaffie

shillyshelly
shelfyshilfyshellyshilly
shelfyshillyshilly
shilfyshellyshelly
shilfyshelfyshelly
shellyfaw
shielyshellyfaw

shilfy
shilfyshelfy shielyshiely
shilfyshelfyshelfy   shielychaffie
chaffiechaffie   chaffiechaffie
chaffiechaffie
shilfyshilfyshilfyshelfyshelfy
chaffieshilfyshilfyshelfyshelfyshelfyshelfy
chaffieshilfyshilfyshelfyshelfyshelfyshelfyshelfy
shilfyshilfyshilfyshelfy   shelfyshelfy
shilfy   shilfy
shilfy
shilfyshelfy

brichtie

Edwin Morgan

Edwin Morgan I was born in Glasgow in 1920. In 2004 I was appointed the first Scots Makar by the Scottish Parliament. All the words here are local terms for 'chaffinch' in various parts of Scotland; I have simply built up my map from their actual geographical distribution. In the title there's a pun on chaffinch/ half-inch – it works in Scots and American though not in English!

In Scotland

The time traivellers' convention

Bring a pairtner tae the Ceilidh
Dress informal, the invite stated
At the time traivellers' convention.

Mary Queen o Scots arrived hersel
Signed up fur speed-datin.
Said she wis a romantic,
Cud lose her heid ower the richt chiel.

The sheik in the tartan troosers
Turned oot tae be Rabbie Burns
Wi a bevy o beauties he'd gaithered
On his traivels.

John Knox tuik charge o the raffle
The kirk being eesed tae collectin
Naebody socht him fur a lady's choice.

Lord Byron niver missed a single dance
In the Gay Gordons. He wis last tae leave.

The Loch Ness Monster, playin watter music
Last seen wis reelin roon bi Ailsa Crag
Wi thirteen kelpies and a Shetlan silkie.

Feedback suggests they'll aa be back neist year.

Sheena Blackhall

Sheena Blackhall I was born and live in Aberdeen. My poems for children are in a pamphlet called *Wizard o the North* and my Scots novella, *Loon*, was published by Itchy Coo. My poems are 'word-pictures', created like an artist paints a portrait, with words instead of oils.

The pizzenous pet shop

The Clarty Cat fae the Western Isles,
Luves tae dive aroon in cundies,
Twice a day fae Mon tae Sat,
But no at aw on Sundays.

The Boakin Budgie flees again!
This time it's had nae seed,
It's stuffed itsel wi fruit an cream,
Tae blaw chunks on yir heid.

The Slevverin Slug is sleekit,
It plans oot its attack,
It slides up yir shirt tae the collar,
An dribbles doon yir back.

The Floater Frog's a minger,
Fowk gie it dug's abuse,
It sneaks up an sooks yir ginger,
An leaves bits in the juice.

The Honkin Hurcheon's hummin,
Its reek ye cannae thole,
It bides beside the cludgie,
An helps clean oot the bowl.

Gregor Steele

Gregor Steele | was born in Motherwell and live in Carluke, South Lanarkshire. A number of my poems appear in *King o the Midden* and *Blethertoun Braes*, collections of 'manky, mingin rhymes in Scots'. Like most of my poems, 'The pizzenous pet shop' was made up partly in the shower, partly when I was out walking or cycling.

Haute, hoat cuisine

Aw, deep-fried Mars,
ah spied ye oan the menu
o ma local chippie.
A speshialtie o Caledonia,
wee, fudgie, chocolate, caramel bar,
ma hert's desire,
bung fu o calories,
cholesterol choked,
cannae whack ye,
a cracker, a stoater.
Unwrapped, in the scud,
belly-flopped in batter
an frazzled tae perfection.

Angela B. Brown

Angela B. Brown Although I live in Edinburgh now, I was born in Dumfries and brought up in Newton Stewart, a small town in Dumfries and Galloway. My poems for children are in my book *Touching Colours*. On the Royal Mile, I pass Bene's fish and chip shop which advertises Deep Fried Mars Bars. Writing the poem in Scots is the best way for me to describe a unique Scottish dessert.

Embra buses

I like tae sit at the front of the bus
and keek through the hole
at the driver's heid.
As he pulls on the wheel
and gives the odd cuss
he disnae ken I'm there.

You can see the hale world fae the tap of a bus:
turbans and burkas, saris wi cardis,
kilts wi Doc Martens,
spiky-haired Goths,
Hoodies and Neds in Burberry caps,
Morningside ladies in sensible hats.

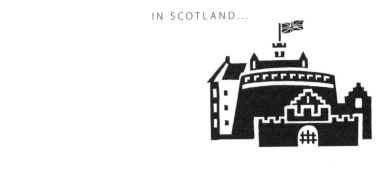

Traffic wardens, grey as sharks
with fluorescent stripes, circle
ready tae strike.
The blind man's dug sits obedient at the kerb,
his flesh flabby.
I'd gie him a guid run.

We stop-start, shoogled aboot in our seats
by traffic cones, road-works,
jaywalkers and drunks.
Crash go the branches
as we lean intae a corner.
Haud tight! Ting! Ting!
We fa doon the stairs.

Stephanie Green

Stephanie Green I was born in Sussex but I now live in Edinburgh. I have written a novel for teenagers called *The Triple Spiral*. It's great fun riding on the top of Embra buses. You get a snapshot of different types of people and a bumpy ride. So writing a poem for me is another kind of snapshot to capture it all.

The Keepie-Uppie King

The Keepie-Uppie King
The Keepie-Uppie King
The Keepie-Uppie
     Keepie-Uppie
     Keepie-Uppie King.

          His robe's a Scotland football top
          his name emblazoned on the back
          his treasure is the football
          he carries inside his pack.

The Keepie-Uppie King
The Keepie-Uppie King
The Keepie-Uppie
     Keepie-Uppie
     Keepie-Uppie King.

          His kingdom is Glasgow's George Square
          his crown, headphones on his head,
          his ball could be a jester's
          with its silver stripes and red.

The Keepie-Uppie King
The Keepie-Uppie King
The Keepie-Uppie
    Keepie-Uppie
    Keepie-Uppie King.

    He holds his subjects in his spell
    flicking the ball from foot to thigh
    to chest to shoulder to neck to head,
    holding court is easy-peasy,
        he doesn't even have to try,
        he doesn't even have to try.

The Keepie-Uppie King
The Keepie-Uppie King
The Keepie-Uppie
    Keepie-Uppie
    Keepie-Uppie King.

Brian Whittingham

Brian Whittingham I was born and live in Glasgow. Once, whilst having a sandwich in Glasgow's George Square, the Keepie-Uppie King appeared and started playing keepie-up. A crowd gathered round him, admiring his skill. He has held the keepie-up record by keeping the ball up thousands of times. He was like a magician on stage, the centre of attention, doing what millions of kids around the world do on a daily basis. I noticed him because I have a curious eye that notices the interesting in everyday life – a must for a poet.

The Isle of Jura

the sound & the silences

the lighthouse & the standing stone

the road & the moor

the fuschia & the hazel

the garden & the beach

the clay pigeons & the wild goats

the peat-bog & the whirlpool

the hotel & the ruin

the ferry & the shingle

the sound & the silences

Ken Cockburn

Ken Cockburn I was born in Kirkcaldy, on the north side of the Firth of Forth, and now live in Edinburgh, on the south side. I don't write many poems for children (except sometimes verses for my daughters' birthdays) but *Write On!: new writing and visual art by young people in Aberdeenshire* contains work from lots of school sessions I ran in 2005. When I went on holiday a few years ago to the island of Islay, I also visited Jura, its smaller, wilder and less populated neighbour. I like to go to new places; the surprises they spring often make me want to write about them, rather than about more familiar places.

*a spurtle

Grandmother

carries the guid Scots tongue in her heid
all the way to London

where it becomes like the kitchen china
worn and cracked with use

kept in the press with the girdle and the spurtle,
the ashet and the jeelie pan.

The good china of English
is what you bring out for visitors:

kept in the cadenza
with the key in its lock.

Lift it carefully on to the silver-plated tray.
Remember which language

you're speaking in. Dinnae –
Dinnae forget.

Elizabeth Burns

Elizabeth Burns I lived in Edinburgh for many years, but have now, like my grandmother, moved to England. My poetry is included in *My Mum's a Punk* and, for older children, in *New Scottish Poetry*. This poem explores how we use English and Scots in different ways and it's also about how things like everyday objects and Scots words, which are often not valued or specially preserved, may easily be lost or forgotten.

On the road

It's nearly New Year and we've loaded the van
with clothes for cold weather, boots and thick socks,
Christmas leftovers, the cat in a box,

and turn to the west. The fields are frozen
but rivers still run to the steely Forth.
The castle at Stirling floats on the carse,

and Ben Ledi's white head shoulders the blue
of a limitless sky. Ben Lomond borrows
light from the loch. At Rest and Be Thankful

the snow picks out the bones of the rock.
The mountains are darker, the sun at their back.
We're over the watershed, down to Cairndow.

Loch Fyne is like glass, and shows us the hills,
the curve of the shore and the lines of black trees
feathered in white, clear and still,

and there on the edge of this world, ourselves.
The wheels revolve, we've chosen the road.
We have to believe that we know where it goes.

Jenni Daiches

Jenni Daiches I was born in Chicago but my parents were Scottish and I have lived in Scotland since 1971. 'On the road' is about a real journey through a winter landscape, from South Queensferry to Ardrishaig in Argyll. The poem started to take shape in my head as we were driving but sometimes months or even years pass before I write about an experience.

Too messy for Nessie

There's a terrible mess
On the shores of Loch Ness
Where the monster's been chucking her bones.
There's bonnets and sporrans
All tattered and torn
And a pile of chewed-up mobile phones.

There's socks and there's shoes
And bits of canoes
And they've turned a bit slimy and green.
There's flippers and goggles
And venture scouts' woggles
And the fins from a small submarine.

There's camera gear
Piled up over years
Rusting away on the shores
And there once lived a man
On the shores in a van
Now all that is left are the doors.

Now you might think Nessie
Is terribly messy
With her rubbish and piles of old bones.
So stop trying to watch her
And stop trying to catch her
It's her place, just leave her alone.

Donald Nelson

Donald Nelson I was born in Glasgow and now live there again after living in many different places. This is only the second poem I have had published, the other was in *Monster Poems*. Sometimes I sit for hours trying to write and nothing happens. This one just came into my head because I was thinking about the mess some people leave behind when they visit beautiful places.

Gazetteer

STROMEFERRY
(NO FERRY)

CARRBRIDGE
(NO BRIDGE)

ULLAPOOL
(NO POOL)

KIRKINTILLOCH
(NO LOCH)

PORTREE
(NO TREE)

GOUROCK
(NO ROCK)

MUIR OF ORD
(NO FORD)

MOTHERWELL
(NO WELL)

DINGWALL
(NO WALL)

STORNOWAY
(NO WAY)

REDPOINT
(NO POINT AT ALL)

AVIEMORE
(NO MORE)

KNOCKANDO
(DO)

Rody Gorman

Rody Gorman I was born in Ireland and now live on the Isle of Skye. I wrote this poem when I was travelling as a passenger to Inverness and passed one of the most famous road signs in the Highlands – 'Stromeferry (no ferry)'. The rest of the poem follows the pattern. Most of my poems are short and do not exceed a page. I've written other poems travelling by car – it's not so easy when you're driving as you have to stop and add hours to your journey.

A Glasgow nonsense rhyme for Molly

Molly Pin Li McLaren,
come home and look
at the pictures in your brand-new book –
a tree, a bird, a fish, a bell,
a bell, a fish, a tree, a bird.
Point, wee Molly, and say the word!

Oh, Molly, I wish
you the moon as white and round as a dish
and a bell, a tree, a bird and a fish.

Touch! Taste! Look! Smell!
(tree, fish, bird, bell)
And listen, wee Molly, listen well
to the wind,
to the wind in the tree go swish
(bird, bell, tree, fish)
to the shrill of the bird and the plop of the fish
and the clang of the bell
and the stories they tell
the stories they tell,
Molly, the tree, the bird, the fish and the bell.

Liz Lochhead

WEE MOLLY was fetched by her new parents, Graham and Julie, from distant Jiang Xi province in China, and came home to Glasgow in time for her first birthday. The city's coat of arms has a tree, a bird, a fish and a bell, hence the traditional –

> *this is the tree that never grew*
> *this is the bird that never flew*
> *this is the fish that never swam*
> *this is the bell that never rang.*

Liz Lochhead This poem was for a real wee girl – Glasgow's newest citizen as she came home from China with her very happy new parents, great friends of mine. I live in Glasgow and was glad for my city that Molly had come to live here too. I find (especially if I've been a bit stuck for a while) that I love writing poems FOR or ABOUT people. Celebrations…

Don't

talk with your mouth full
leave the table without asking
speak to your mother like that
let the sun go down on your wrath
forget to write
go

without saying goodbye

Helena Nelson

Helena Nelson I was born in Cheshire but I've lived in Fife for nearly thirty years. I am interested in the words and phrases we remember all our lives (even when we don't want to). My grandmother, for example, always used to say, 'Never let the sun go down on your wrath', while my mother used to say (among other things), 'Don't speak to your father like *that*'. When you're a kid, people are always telling you what not to do. One day I was thinking about all these negative instructions – '*don't* do this' and '*don't* do that' – and out of that thought came this poem. It starts in a bossy voice but it ends in a sad one.

My mum's sari

I love my mother's sari on the washing line
Flapping like a giant flag, which I pretend is mine.

I love its silky softness when it's folded to a square
Which I can roll into a ball and pretend it isn't there.

I love to hold its free bit that swings over mum's back
And wrap it round my shoulders, like a potato in a sack.

I love the pleats that fall in shape and spread out like a fan
Where my kid brother crouches and says 'catch me if you can.'

I love to wash my dirty hands at the kitchen sink
And wipe them on mum's sari before she can even blink.

But when she takes her *anchal* and ties it round her waist
I know it's time for battle and a quick escape is best!

Bashabi Fraser

(THE ANCHAL is the free bit at the end of the sari that is slung over the shoulder)

Bashabi Fraser I was born in West Bengal in India and now I divide my life between the two countries I love most – India and Britain. After living in London, I returned to India to attend a convent school on the Himalayas where I was threatened with expulsion after breaking all possible rules! I have published children's stories and written a shadow puppet play and I am a classical Indian dancer and choreographer.

Feart

In the pit mirk nicht at the fit o the stairs,
A heard a wee noise that jist made the hairs,
oan the back o ma neck, staun straight up oan end
ma teeth start tae chatter, ma hert fair bend.

A cocked ma lugs an strained fir tae hear.
Wis it ghaists or folk? Wir they faur or near?
Wid they be freenly craturs or murderers foul?
Wir they here fir a blether or a bluidthirsty prowl?

Wi a flash o lichtnin, an a rattle o thunner,
the storm fair brewed an A coontit tae a hunner.
Then A gaithert ma courage an stertit tae climb
When oot o the shaddas twae fit at a time,

A wee black baw o fur an fluff
Came trottin doon the stairs, fair in a huff.
Ma new wee kitten jist gied me a look,
an walkt strecht past, fair famisht fir her food.

Liz Niven

Liz Niven I was born in Glasgow and now live in Dumfries. I have edited a collection of short stories for children called *A Braw Brew*, some short plays for young people and some English textbooks for secondary schools. I wrote 'Feart' for some very wee Primary Ones because they were doing scary poems. Also, I'd just got a tiny new black kitten who used to frighten everybody by arriving unexpectedly out of dark corners. He was watching me while I wrote this! It's ordinary, everyday events that make me want to write a new poem — the sort of recognisable things that happen to all of us.

Above Daldowie, 1990

Gran is a bird.

Ten years it took
for the dragging flesh to dissolve
and the bones to grow thin and light.

Her hands curled to slow claws
below translucent skin.

The gold ring on her finger
slipped away
and was replaced with plastic
round her wrist
in case she flew too soon.

Far beyond words and Maltesers
she shed her teeth
leaving a small dark hole
below a sharpening beak.

At the end
her wings were hidden,
small but folded
below the sheet.

Only the regular lifting
of her shoulder
showed preparations were complete.

And now, she's spread her wings
and flown away
free as a wraith of white smoke
free as a bird.

Valerie Thornton

Valerie Thornton I was born in Glasgow, brought up in Stirling and now live in Glasgow again. I write poems and short stories and have just finished a school book called *The Writer's Craft*. Daldowie is a crematorium and I tried to ease the pain of my gran's death, at the age of ninety-eight, by writing this poem in which she rises above death.

Murphy

Black as the core of a shadow

Soft as a 'can't afford' fleece

Warm as the 'time to get up now'

Safe as yourself, only safer

Loving as only dogs can

Karen Doherty

Karen Doherty I was born in Fife, on the east coast of Scotland. My books for children include *Threat – a story of Mary Slessor* and *Murderers – a story of Burke and Hare*. The poem 'Murphy' was written because sometimes the most ordinary things are the most special.

MY DAD SAYS

My dad says I'm a pest.
He says I'm a fusspot
I'm a whinger
I'm a pain in the neck
I'm a bottomless pit
I'm too big for my boots
I'm a thorn in his flesh.

My dad says
I'm an empty vessel
I'm an accident waiting to happen.
He says I'm a jinx and a minx
And I'm lazy and mean –
I'm a prima donna
I'm a wimp
I'm a soap opera queen.

Sometimes my dad says I'm mad.
But my mum says –
I'm just like my dad!

Magi Gibson

Magi Gibson I was brought up in a small town just outside Glasgow. My poems appear in several anthologies for children and I've just finished a novel for young adults. When I was wee, I was always being told I was just like my dad – which is a bit troubling for a girl. I didn't want big muscly arms and a beard. I suppose that must be why I wrote the poem but, to be honest, the first lines just popped into my head one day and the rest of the poem tumbled out after. I wrote the lines down then jiggled them about to get the rhythms as strong as possible.

No.115 dreams

The living room remembers gran dancing to Count Basie.
The kitchen can still hear my aunts fighting on Christmas day.
The hall is worried about the loose banister.
The small room is troubled by the missing hamster.
The toilet particularly dislikes my grandfather.
The wallpaper covers up for the whole family.

And No.115 dreams of lovely houses by the sea.
And No.115 dreams of one night in the country.

The stairs are keeping schtum about the broken window.
The toilet's sick of the trapped pipes squealing so.
The walls aren't thick enough for all the screaming.
My parent's bedroom has a bed in a choppy sea.
My own bedroom loves the bones of me.
My brother's bedroom needs a different boy.

And No.115 dreams of yellow light, an attic room.
And No.115 dreams of a chimney, a new red roof.

And the red roof dreams of robin redbreasts
tap dancing on the red dance floor in the open air.

Jackie Kay

Jackie Kay I was born in Edinburgh and brought up in Glasgow. I have written four books for children so far. The latest two are called *The Frog Who Dreamed She Was an Opera Singer* and *Strawgirl*. I now live with my son in Manchester. For this poem, I was trying to imagine what it would be like if every room in a house had feelings and secret emotions.

Sometimes

In
all
the
rush
and
hurry
of
our
lives
we
need
so
much
just
now
and
then
to
find
an

island

Kenneth Steven

Kenneth Steven I have grown up in Highland Perthshire. My first collection of poems for children, *Imagining Things*, was composed in my writing cabin in Aberfeldy. There, the only thing I can hear is birdsong.

Spell of the bridge

Hold the wish on your tongue
As you cross
What the bridge cannot hear
Cannot fall

For the river would carry
Your hopes to the sea
To the net of a stranger
To the silt bed of dreams

Hold the wish on your tongue
As you cross
And on the far side
Let the wish go first

Helen Lamb

Helen Lamb The River Allan flows through the town of Dunblane, where I grew up. There were four bridges across the river but only one wishing bridge. You made a wish then held your breath as you ran across.

Sorry

I'm sorry I spilled the jug of milk
I'm sorry I banged the front door
I'm sorry turquoise isnae quite green
I'm sorry my dog peed on your floor

I'm sorry I forgot your birthday
I'm sorry I really really meant to call
I'm sorry I couldn't spell Pharaoh
And didn't know the capital of Nepal

I'm sorry this soup is too salty
I'm sorry your toast is burned
I'm sorry for the crumbs on the sofa
I'm sorry these gloves are seal fur

I'm sorry for Flodden and Culloden
I'm sorry for Genghis Khan
I'm sorry for locking myself out
I'm sorry I'm not Spiderman

I'm sorry I missed the penalty
I'm sorry I didn't make the catch
I'm sorry the pies all ran out
At the last Queen of the South fitba match

I'm sorry the world is starving
I'm sorry I didn't finish my sprouts
I'm sorry I'm full of Irn-Bru
I'm sorry I wear my pants inside out

I'm sorry for hunching my shoulders
I'm sorry for my glo[tt]al stop
I'm sorry Elvis never sang in Scotland
I'm sorry for the whole damn lot

I'm sorry I forgot to brush my teeth
I'm sorry for the ozone layer
I'm sorry for the space I take up –
But you know none of this seems fair

For none of us can live our lives
Spending half of them on our knees
If we were so frightened of doing things wrong
We'd never've come down from the trees

So let's have a bonfire of the sorries
We keep on the tips of our tongues
Let's grow up proud and straight and true
And not be so afraid of offending our mums.

Tom Pow

Tom Pow I was born in Edinburgh but I've lived in Dumfries for many years. Robert Burns is buried here and J. M. Barrie (author of *Peter Pan*) went to school here. My son, Cameron, and I are keen Queen of the South football supporters. I've written three picture books for children – *Callum's Big Day*, *Who is the World For?* and *Tell Me One Thing, Dad* – and three novels for young adults. My friend, the poet Alastair Reid, told me that when he brought his son, Jasper, to Scotland when Jasper was a boy, he kept asking, 'Why does everyone say sorry all the time?' Why do we? Even when people bump into *us*!

Mise agus Pangur Bàn

Tha dàn Èireannach às an 9mh linn a' toirt dealbh dhuinn air cat, Pangur Bàn,
agus a mhaighstir, is gach fear aca gu comhartail an sàs san alt aige fhèin –
sealg luchan agus sealg fhreagairtean a rèir a chèile.

Chunnaic am manach gum b' iomchaidh
Pangur Bàn a bhith ri luchan
fhad 's a bha e fhèin ri sgrìobhadh
sa scriptorium fhuar is luchan rim fògradh.

Ach chan eil an gnothach cho sìmplidh
dhomhsa is an cat làn Whiskas is dallag aige.
An leig mi leis a' chat cluich le a chreich
is sin na dhualchas,

No an glac mi an creutair sgeunach san t-sluasaid
ach an tilg mi a-mach e san fheur fhada riaslach
far an ruith e air falbh gus an tèid a ghlacadh . . .
is truas dham cho-chreutair san nàdar agamsa?

Nam bu dualach e do Phangur Bàn
greimeachadh air an luch a dh'aona leum
tha e dualach dhomhsa
a bhith eadar dà bharail:

An-dè 's ann a shàbhail mi an luch;
an-diugh toilichidh mi an cat, 's mi sgìth . . .
O nan robh am breithneachadh ceart
mar bu dual do mhac-an-duine.

Meg Bateman

Meg Bateman Rugadh mi ann an Dùn Èideann. Tha mi a-nis a' fuireach san Eilean Sgitheanach còmhla ri cus chat. Sgrìobh mi an dàn seo mar fhreagairt do dhàn a chaidh a dhèanamh do chat anns an 9mh linn le manach Èireannach. Bha am manach air a dhòigh ghlan gu robh am cat, Pangur Bàn, an tòir air luchagan fhad 's a bha esan an tòir air eòlas, ach, mar a chì thu, cha robh a' cheist cho sìmplidh dhòmhsa...

The monk and Pangur Bàn

A ninth-century Irish poem describes a cat, Pangur Bàn, and his master companionably intent on what each does best – hunting mice and intellectual solutions respectively.

The monk saw it fitting
that Pangur Bàn should be busy with a mouse
while he was busy with writing
in a cold scriptorium with mice to keep down.

But the matter is not so simple for me
when the cat has a shrew and is full of Whiskas.
Should I leave the cat well alone
as playing with his prey is part of his nature,

Or should I shovel up the terrified shrew
and throw it out in the long grass
to scuttle away till next it's caught . . .
as compassion for others is part of mine?

As it was instinctive for Pangur Bàn
to leap on his prey at one swift bound,
so is it instinctive for me
to hover between two minds:

Yesterday I saved the mouse,
today, being tired, I'll please the cat . . .
If only hitting on the right judgement
were instinctive to humankind!

Meg Bateman

Meg Bateman I was born in Edinburgh and now live on the Isle of Skye with too many cats. I wrote this poem in contrast to a poem written about a cat by an Irish monk in the ninth century. The monk is perfectly happy about his cat, Pangur Bàn, trapping mice while he traps knowledge. But, as you see, the situation for me was not so simple . . .

from *The Book of Why?*

Why doesn't a chair fly?
Why do we have tongues?
Why are the stars so silver?
Why do girls wear bobbles?
Why do boys try and do handstands?
Why are there earrings in the world?
Why is sherbet so tickly on your tongue?
Why can you hear the wind, but not see it?
Why have old people got see-through skin?
Why can't you choose what you were born like?
Why do our voices sound different to each other?
Why do people breathe a lot when they are excited?
Why is the sky blue, when the surface of the air is clear?

Alec Finlay

Alec Finlay I am a poet, artist and publisher, born in Inverness in 1966. This is a *found* poem I composed from questions that were asked by children aged three to five years. They are selected from the Archive of *The Book of Questions*, an ongoing and endless project; go to You Are Invited on www.alecfinlay.com for details. I have a number of other projects made for and with children, such as *Wordwood*, *Three Rivers Crossword* and *Hyakuin Renga*.

: – (

Can't spell, won't spell

(On hearing of the new Scots Spellchecker programme, 'Canny Scot')

CANNAE SPELL, WINNAE SPELL – lay it oan thi line:
when it come tae orthaegraphic skills this laddie disnae shine.
Eh cannae spell 'MaGonnagal', Eh cannae spell 'Renaissence' –
hoo Eh feel aboot this flaw is becummin raw complaysance.
If Eh cannae spell in English dae Eh huvtae spell in Scots?
Is meh joattur filled wi crosses when thi proablem is wir nots?
Wir not a singul naishun and therr's not a singul tongue:
we talk wan wey gin wir aalder and anither if wir young;
we talk diffrent in thi Borders than we dae up in thi Broch;
wir meenisters talk funny when they skate oan frozen lochs.
Huv ye seen hoo Lech Walensa's Roabin Wulliums wi a tash?
Huv ye noticed hoo Pat Lally's kinna nippy wi thi cash?
Well yi widnae if yir sittan wi yir heid stuck til a screen
trehin tae spell oot whit ye think insteid o seyin whit ye mean.

: ¬D

W. N. Herbert

W. N. Herbert I was born in Dundee and grew up in a bungalow in Broughty Ferry on the Firth of Tay. I now live just outside Newcastle in a lighthouse in North Shields, which is on the mouth of the Tyne. I wrote 'Can't spell, won't spell' because there are a couple of tricky words that, no matter how I try, I can't spell correctly. This made me think of all the words we use in Scotland which they don't use in England. These may appear to be spelt wrongly but they're not – they're just spelt differently. So then I thought, rather than tidy Scots words up and make them like English words, maybe it would be better to leave them alone and let them be tricky.

the panel

horsefly

packhorse

backpack

fight back

bun fight

currant bun

blackcurrant

pot black

teapot

China tea

bone china

whalebone

whale

ller whale

killer whale

Roundabout

...ing round

Roundabout

about-turn

turntable

tabletop

top dog

dogfish

fish finger

finger paint

paintbrush

brushwood

woodwind

windmill

millpond

pondweed

weedkill...

Julia Donaldson

Julia Donaldson I grew up in London but I now live in Glasgow. I have written picture books such as *The Gruffalo* and older children's books such as *The Giants and the Joneses*. 'Roundabout' is really more of a game than a poem; I like playing with words and I hope that readers will enjoy playing the game and making up their own word chains or circles.

Cat food rap

Well the moggy strolled in wi somehn clamped in its jaws.
It laid doon its present, an it waited for applause.
But the cratur wisni deid, and it struggled tae its feet,
an A wis fair amazed when it stertit ti speak:

'Hiya, A'm a fairy, look, here's ma pointy hat,
an A'd like ti show A'm grateful that ye saved me fae the cat,
well A widni tell a lee, an A'm no on the fiddle,
A'll gie ye a reward if ye can guess ma riddle.

'Can ye show me the ram, that disnae hiv a fleece?
Can you show me chips, that were never fried in grease?
Tell me where are the windaes nae sun shines through?
And where is the moose, that never ever grew?'

Well I gave the fairy answers, cos I wanted her prize.
Tellt her, 'Chips urni greasy till ye turn them inti fries.
A ram has nae fleece once the shepherd's yased his cutter,
and nae sun comes in the windae if ye jist close the shutter.

'And when two wee mooses really love yin anither,
Well their wean is jist an egg till it grows in its mither.
So there ye hiv yer answers, and A think it a' fits
so jist gie me ma reward, an that's us quits.'

Well the fairy says, 'Son, nae reward for you the night,
ye think ye're awfy clever, but yer answer isni right.
The answer's a computer, whit d'ye say ti that?'
Well, A lifted up the fairy, an A fed her tae the cat.

Anne Armstrong

Anne Armstrong I live in the depths of Lanarkshire. My cat often brings me presents of food – no fairies so far, though. Another poet challenged me to write a poem based on a riddle. This poem is the result. I like to compose poems on my computer because it's easy to change them around. I use an on-line rhyming dictionary.

The Old Poet

an t-seann bhàrd
a' faireachdainn sreath
a' tighinn air
mean air mhean
mar sreathart

the old poet
feels a line
coming on him
little by little
like a sneeze

Kevin MacNeil
(after Paul Claudel)

aaaaaaaaaaaaaaaaaachoo

Kevin MacNeil I was born and raised in Stornoway on the Isle of Lewis. I write poems, plays, novels and songs in English and Gaelic. I believe anyone who wants to can become a writer – and that includes you!

Brekin rainbows

He wis just a wee lad
dibblin in a puddle,
glaur fae heid tae fit,
enjoyin haen a guddle.
He micht hae bin a poacher
puin salmon fae the beck.
He coulda bin a paratrooper,
swamp up tae his neck.
Mibbe he wis brekin rainbows
reflectit in the watter,
his ill-shod feet wid split the prism
an mak the colours scatter.
Onywey he wis faur awa,
deep wandert in his dreams;
it richt sobert me tae mind
a dub's no whit it seems.
An while ah watched an grieved
the loss that maks a man a mug,
alang the road fair breenged his maw
an skelpt him roon the lug.

Janet Paisley

Janet Paisley I live in a small village in the middle of Scotland. Most of my poems and stories for children are written for radio or TV but some are in books like this one. I wrote this poem when I found out it's not so much fun splashing in puddles if nobody gets annoyed about it. But I still keep my wellies handy, just in case.

Russian doll

You wid tink dey wir only ee dolly   *there was, one*
sheeny an painted an bricht,
triggit up i da flags o aa nations: *dressed up*
but some rippit – dat canna be richt?   *torn*

Inside dat der a Wast European   *that, there is*
wi a luik less uncan ta see.   *foreign*
You can tell fae da een der a blydeness   *eyes, gladness*
dat life's wirt livin an free.

Inside dat een you'll fin yet anidder   *another*
jöst as boannie but peerier scale.   *just, smaller*
Dat's da British identity hoidin: *hiding*
göd ta delicht in as weel.   *good*

Inside dat een a Scot is hunkered   *crouching*
wi a baetin haert prood ta belang
tae a country still writin hits story,
transformin wi poems an sang.

Inside dat een, a ting o a dolly   *tiny wee*
wi a tongue tied ta love o a laand:
tae an ain place, an ain fock, a language   *own folk*
ta hadd i da löf o a haand.   *hold, the palm*

Inside dat een, da mintiest dukkie: *tiniest dolly*
but da key tae dem aa, jöst da sam.
Hit waels aa da tochts, aa da feelins   *sifts all, thoughts*
sae da inner an ooter is wan.   *outer are one*

Christine De Luca

Christine De Luca I was born in Waas, Shetland, but live in Edinburgh. I have written some poems
for children, both in English and Shetland dialect, but more recently, as part of a small cooperative, have
produced children's storybooks and CDs in dialect. I wrote this poem in response to the current debate about
identity – just because we're Scottish surely doesn't mean we can't be enthusiastic British or European or
world citizens . . . or celebrate belonging to a small village or parish?

Hiding places

The world beneath the table
When no one knows you're there,
The second home that's all your own
Underneath the stair.

Your bedroom when you shut the door
And in the mirror see
This quite fantastic person who
You know you're going to be.

The space above the wardrobe where
Your best-kept secrets nest,
The attic that's a hideout when
Your parent is a pest.

The hideaway inside your head
Contains a magic light,
Just switch it on and you can zap
All monsters of the night.

A person needs a hiding place –
Four walls alone won't do.
You need a corner, secret, quiet,
to grow you into you.

Diana Hendry

Diana Hendry I live near the Botanic Gardens in Edinburgh. I like writing stories and poems for children of all ages. My favourite book is *Harvey Angell*. This poem began with a memory of the hiding place under the stairs in my childhood home and later hiding in my bedroom and secretly scribbling stories. I think I still like hiding!

afternoord

Galumph

A gallop which ends
in tragedy, as it trips
over its own feet

Andrew McCallum

Andrew McCallum Hi! I'm fae Biggar and I wrote this poem for a laugh. It's a haiku, which is a Japanese kind of poem, and it's about the sound the word 'gallop' makes when it crashes.

scots

a

abune above
ashet an oval serving plate or pie dish

b

bents grass-covered dunes by the sea
blether a chat; to chat
boakin vomiting
braes hills
breenged rushed
brekin breaking

c

chiel a young man
clarty dirty
cludgie a lavatory
cuddie a horse
cundies drains

d

drookit drenched
dub a puddle
dug a dog

e

een eyes
eesed used (to)

f

flee fly
frae from
freenly friendly

g

gang go
girdle an iron plate used for baking
girns traps
glaur mud, slime
Glesca Glasgow
greet to weep
guddle a mess
guid good

h

haein a crack having a chat
heid head
hurcheon a hedgehog

i

ile oil

j

jeelie jam

words

k

keek peek
kelpie a horse-shaped water demon

l

leddie lady
lugs ears

m

minger a disgusting person
mirk the dark
mune the moon

n

neb a nose

o

oxters armpits

p

pechin gasping
puggled exhausted

s

sark a shirt
shoon shoes
silkie a mythological seal-creature
skelpt slapped
sleekit cunning
slevverin dribbling
sooks sucks
spurtle a short stick for stirring porridge
staun stand
stoater a smasher

t

Tinto a prominent hill in Lanarkshire

w

wobat a woolly bear

u

unner under

y

yird earth

acknowledgements

OUR THANKS ARE DUE to the following authors and publishers who have given permission to include or reproduce works:

Poems by Anne Armstrong, Meg Bateman, Sheena Blackhall, Angela B. Brown, Tom Bryan, Eunice M. Buchanan, Elizabeth Burns, John Burnside, Gerry Cambridge, Thomas A. Clark, Ken Cockburn, Robert Crawford, Jenni Daiches, Christine De Luca, Karen Doherty, Carol Ann Duffy, Richard Edwards, Alec Finlay, Matthew Fitt, Bashabi Fraser, Robin Fulton, Magi Gibson, Valerie Gillies, John Glenday, Stephanie Green, Mandy Haggith, Diana Hendry, Jackie Kay, Helen Lamb, Joan Lennon, Liz Lochhead, Andrew McCallum, James McGonigal, Richard Medrington, Elspeth Murray, Donald Nelson, Helena Nelson, Liz Niven, Janet Paisley, Tom Pow, Chris Powici, Richard Price, Tessa Ransford, James Robertson, Dilys Rose, Alan Spence, Gregor Steele, Ian Stephen, Valerie Thornton, Brian Whittingham and Fiona Wilson are by kind permission of the authors.

'Roundabout' taken from *Crazy Mayonnaisy Mum* by Julia Donaldson © Julia Donaldson 2004, published by Macmillan Children's Books, London, UK; 'Protectit Bird' by Duncan Glen from *Collected Poems 1965-2005* (Kirkcaldy: Akros, 2006) is reprinted by permission of Akros Publications; 'Gazetteer' by Rody Gorman from *Air a' Charbad fo Thalamh/On the Underground* (Edinburgh: Polygon, 2000) is reproduced by permission of Polygon, an imprint of Birlinn Ltd; 'Can't Spell, Won't Spell' by W. N. Herbert from *The Big Bumper Book of Troy* (Tarset: Bloodaxe, 2002) is reprinted by permission of Bloodaxe Books Ltd; from 'After Paul Claudel' from *Love and Zen in the Outer Hebrides* by Kevin MacNeil, first published in Great Britain by Canongate Books Ltd, 14 High Street, Edinburgh EH1 1TE, is reprinted by permission of Canongate Books Ltd; 'The Chaffinch Map of Scotland' by Edwin Morgan from *Collected Poems* (Manchester: Carcanet, 1990) is reprinted by permission of Carcanet Press Ltd; 'What the Horses See at Night' from *Swithering* by Robin Robertson (London: Picador, 2006) is reprinted by permission of Macmillan, London, UK; extract taken from *Imagining Things* by Kenneth Steven, published by Lion Hudson plc, 2005, copyright © 2005 Kenneth Steven, used with permission of Lion Hudson plc.

'Hiding Places' by Diana Hendry and 'No. 115 Dreams' by Jackie Kay were commissioned and first published by the Scottish Poetry Library in the 'Poet in the House' teachers' resource pack for the 2004 Poetry & Architecture Schools' Poetry Competition.

'The pluffman' by Gerry Cambridge was first published in *Stepping into the Avalanche* (Biggar: Brownsbank Press, 2003); 'My mum's sari' by Bashabi Fraser was first published in *Poems Out Loud*, selected by Brian Moses (London: Hodder Wayland, 2003); 'Spell of the bridge' by Helen Lamb was first published in *Going up Ben Nevis in a Bubble Car (New Writing Scotland 18)*, edited by Moira Burgess and Janet Paisley (Glasgow: ASLS, 2001); 'Five Fish' by Ian Stephen was first commissioned by the composer David P. Graham, set to music by him and performed by the Schedrik-Chor, conducted by Pavel Brochin, in Bonn, Germany, June 2005.

Copyright of 'From Hereabout Hill' by Seán Rafferty belongs to Farms for City Children.